HISTORY & GEO NORTH AMERICA

MW01227012

NORTH AMERICA

Introduction |3

1. Geography 4
Land, Lakes, and Rivers |6
Peninsulas, Oceans, and Islands |10
Other Facts |14
Self Test 1 |19

2. Northern Countries 22
Greenland |23
Canada |26
United States |33
States and Capitals Test |55
Self Test 2 |56

3. Southern Countries 59
Mexico |60
Central America |62
West Indies |66
Self Test 3 |71

LIFEPAC Test |Pull-out

Author:
Theresa K. Buskey, B.A., J.D.

Editor:
Alan Christopherson, M.S.

Assistant Editor:
Annette M. Walker, B.S.

Media Credits:
Page 3: © 1xpert, iStock,Thinkstock; **4:** © alehnia, iStock, Thinkstock; **6:** © Oleg Fedorkin, Hemera, Thinkstock; **7:** © WerksMedia, iStock, Thinkstock; **8:** © Ricardo Reitmeyer, iStock, Thinkstock; © Jim Pintar, iStock, Thinkstock; **11:** © Stocktrek Images, Thinkstock © devans1, iStock, Thinkstock, © shalamov, iStock, Thinkstock; **13:** © JPaulB, iStock, Thinkstock; **15:** © venturecx, iStock, Thinkstock, © Dodge65, iStock, Thinkstock; © jvdwolf, iStock, Thinkstock; **17:** © Mike Watson Images, iStock, Thinkstock; **22:** © Stockbyte, Thinkstock; **24:** © Enrique Jggarcia, iStock, Thinkstock; **25:** © Henri Vdl, iStock, Thinkstock; **27:** © Androsov, iStock, Thinkstock; © Purestock, Thinkstock; **29:** © Hemera Technologies, AbleStock.com, Thinkstock; **30:** © Vladone, iStock, Thinkstock; **31:** © Bee Creative, iStock, Thinkstock; © ErikaMitchell, iStock, Thinkstock; **32, 36, 40:** © Dorling Kindersley, Thinkstock; **37:** © DebraMillet, Thinkstock; **41:** © Livinus, iStock, Thinkstock; **44:** © Linda Parton, iStock, Thinkstock; **46:** © prudkov, iStock, Thinkstock; **48:** © kojihirano, iStock, Thinkstock; **51:** © theartist312, iStock, Thinkstock; **59:** © Bill Berry Photography, iStock, Thinkstock; **61:** © dubassy, iStock, Thinkstock; **64:** © Castillo Dominici, iStock, Thinkstock; **67:** © fatchoi, iStock, Thinkstock; **67:** © brocreative, iStock, Thinkstock.

All maps in this book © Image Resources, unless otherwise stated.

Alpha Omega
PUBLICATIONS

804 N. 2nd Ave. E.
Rock Rapids, IA 51246-1759

NORTH AMERICA

This **LIFEPAC®** will teach the basic geography of North America. This will require you to memorize many names and places. You will learn the features of the continent and the countries. Then, when there is an oil spill near the Aleutian Islands, a volcanic eruption in Honduras, or a shipwreck near the Bahamas, you will know what the news reporter is talking about. You will also learn your U.S. states and capitals in this LIFEPAC. Many of the terms you have used this year will be reviewed and used to identify places on the continent. Places you need to be able to find on a map will be <u>underlined</u>. So, sharpen your brain and start learning your way around North America!!

Objectives

Read these objectives. The objectives tell you what you will be able to do when you have successfully completed this LIFEPAC. Each section will list according to the numbers below what objectives will be met in that section. When you have finished this LIFEPAC, you should be able to:

1. Name and find on a map many of the geographic features of North America.
2. Name the major countries/regions of North America.
3. Name the states on a blank map of the United States.
4. Match U.S. states and their capitals.
5. Tell about the geography, history, and people of the major countries/regions of North America.
6. Recognize the names of the countries of Central America.
7. Recognize the names of the major islands of the West Indies.

1. GEOGRAPHY

North America is the third largest continent on earth. It stretches from inside the Arctic Circle to a point only 700 miles (1,126 km) from the equator. It is shaped sort of like a big triangle balanced on one corner. The continent includes Greenland, Canada, the United States, Mexico, Central America (the countries south of Mexico), and the West Indies. The map on the next page shows the size, shape, and many of the important features of North America.

Objectives

Review these objectives. When you have completed this section, you should be able to:

1. Name and find on a map many of the geographic features of North America.
2. Name the major countries/regions of North America.
5. Tell about the geography, history, and people of the major countries/regions of North America.

Vocabulary

Study these new words. Learning the meanings of these words is a good study habit and will improve your understanding of this LIFEPAC.

abundance (ə bun′ dəns). Great plenty; quantity that is more than enough.

cordillera (kôr′ dil yâr′ ə). A group of mountain ranges, often consisting of a number of parallel chains. Usually the largest group on a continent.

heritage (her′ ə tij). What is handed down from one generation to the next.

lock (lok). The part of a canal in which the level of the water can be changed by letting water in or out, to raise or lower ships.

mainland (mān′ land). The main part of a continent or country, not including islands or small peninsulas.

migrate (mī′ grāt). To move from one place to settle in another.

overwhelm (ō′ vər hwelm′). To crush or defeat; overcome completely.

province (prov′ ins). One of the main divisions of a country.

range (rānj). A row or line of mountains.

source (sôrs). A person or place from which anything comes or is obtained.

Note: *All vocabulary words in this LIFEPAC appear in* **boldface** *print the first time they are used. If you are unsure of the meaning when you are reading, study the definitions given.*

Pronunciation Key: hat, āge, cãre, fär; let, ēqual, tėrm; it, īce; hot, ōpen, ôrder; oil; out; cup, pùt, rüle; child; long; thin; /ᵺH/ for then; /zh/ for measure; /u/ or /ə/ represents /a/ in about, /e/ in taken, /i/ in pencil, /o/ in lemon, and /u/ in circus.

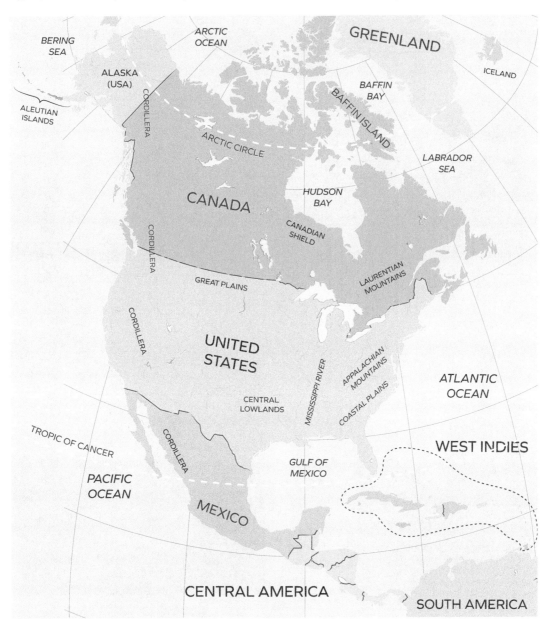

| North America with its major features

Land, Lakes, and Rivers

The Land. North America has a set of mountain **ranges** on both sides and a large plain in the center. All along western (left, on a map) Canada and the United States are a group of mountains called the **cordillera**. These mountains continue south to cover most of Mexico and Central America. On the eastern (right) side of Canada and the U.S. is another set of mountain ranges, the Appalachian Mountains and Laurentian Mountains. The Appalachians are south of the St. Lawrence River, while the Laurentians are to the north. Between the eastern and western mountain ranges spreads a huge, fertile plain.

The cordillera are better known by the names given to the different ranges. The Rocky Mountains are probably the best known range in the American cordillera. They are the mountains that seem to spring up out of the Great Plains when you travel west across America. Even further west, there are other ranges along the Pacific coast. Between the Rocky Mountains and the coastal mountains is the Great Basin.

The Great Basin is a desert area of bowl-shaped plateaus between the mountains. It is a desert because the mountains block moisture from getting there. Any rain that does fall there is likely to be trapped in the bottom, like a basin, which gives the area its name.

In Mexico the cordillera form three ranges, called the Sierra Madre. The Sierra Madre Occidental are along the west coast, while the Sierra Madre Oriental are along the east coast. In the south is the Sierra Madre Del Sur. Between all of the mountain ranges is a plateau, where most of the people of Mexico live.

The eastern mountains are not as tall as the cordillera. The White, Green, Blue Ridge, and Great Smoky Mountains are part of the Appalachians, which stretch from Maine to Alabama. The European colonists who settled the Atlantic coast had to cross these mountains to reach the American frontier. The difficult traveling kept most Americans along the east coast until after the Revolutionary War. The

| The Great Basin includes Death Valley

Canadian part of the eastern highlands is called the Laurentian Mountains. They run near the Atlantic coast north of the St. Lawrence River.

So, the mountains to remember are the cordillera on the west (left) side of the continent, which include the Rocky Mountains in the U.S. and the Sierra Madre in Mexico; and on the east (right) side, the Appalachians in the U.S. and the Laurentians in Canada.

| The Great Smoky Mountains

Choose the correct word to complete these sentences.

1.1   The group of mountains along the western (Pacific) side of North America are

called the _____ .

1.2   The eastern mountains are the _____ Mountains in

Canada and the _____ Mountains in the United States.

1.3   The desert area in the center of the cordillera in the United States is called the

_____ .

1.4   The cordillera in Mexico are called the _____ .

1.5   The best known range of the cordillera in the United States is the

_____ Mountains.

The plains between the eastern and western mountains are divided into three parts. The northern part is the Canadian Shield. (Also called the Laurentian Plateau). It is a plateau of rock that runs across northern Canada, around Hudson Bay, and as far south as the Great Lakes. There are many rivers which can be used for hydroelectric power. The soil is thin and not very good for crops, but the rocks are rich in mineral resources.

| The Great Plains

The southern part of the plains is the Central Lowlands. The western side, near the cordillera, is called the Great Plains. The Great Plains run from central Canada to Texas. It is a grassland of rich soil that gets drier the further west it goes.

Besides the eastern mountains, the cordillera, the Canadian Shield, the Great Plains, and the Central Lowlands, there is one other area of you should know. That is the Coastal Plains of the east. They run along the Atlantic coast in the United States and around the Gulf of Mexico. This area was quickly settled by the Europeans. It has good farmland, and rivers for transportation. This is where thirteen British colonies formed a new nation they called the United States of America.

Lakes and Rivers. South of the Canadian Shield are five large lakes called the Great Lakes. They are on the border between Canada and the United States. Lake Superior, the largest freshwater lake in the world, is the one farthest to the west. Then comes Lake Michigan (the only one completely inside the United States), Lake Huron, Lake Erie, and Lake Ontario.

A system of rivers, canals, and **locks** connects all of the Great Lakes. They are also connected to the St. Lawrence River, which flows to the Atlantic Ocean. The whole system is called the St. Lawrence Seaway, because it allows ocean ships to sail into the center of the continent. This means that cities like Detroit, Chicago, Toronto, and Montreal are ocean port cities even though they are far inland.

| A light house on Lake Superior

The great <u>Mississippi River</u> system flows through the Great Plains and the Central Lowlands into the Gulf of Mexico. It draws water from the streams of both the Rocky and the Appalachian Mountains! The mighty Mississippi has allowed people to travel and trade by using riverboats, long before good roads were built.

There are many other rivers and lakes in North America, but the Great Lakes, the Mississippi River, and the St. Lawrence are the ones you must know for this LIFEPAC.

Choose the correct word to complete these sentences.

1.6 The northern part of the plains is called the _____ , a plateau of rock.

1.7 Lake _____ is the largest lake in the world.

1.8 The names of the Great Lakes are: _____ ,

_____ , _____ , _____ ,

and _____ .

1.9 The St. Lawrence Seaway connects the _____ Ocean with the

_____ Lakes.

1.10 The great river system of the Central Lowlands is the _____

River system.

1.11 The United States was founded on the _____ Plains.

1.12 The Mississippi River system empties into the Gulf of _____ .

Peninsulas, Oceans, and Islands

The map of North America shows the major oceanside features of North America. Many of these are easy to remember if you can connect them with something nearby. The Gulf of California, for example, is south of California. The Gulf of Mexico is next to Mexico. Find little tricks and hints to help you remember each place and its name.

There are three important peninsulas you need to know. Baja California is the name of the Mexican peninsula that extends south of the state of California. It is a long, narrow, mountainous finger of land. The Florida Peninsula is easy: it is the state of Florida. The Yucatán Peninsula is on the southeast side of Mexico on the Gulf of

| North America

Mexico. It divides the Gulf of Mexico from the Caribbean Sea. It was the home of an ancient Indian civilization called the Maya. Today the ruins of their cities are a tourist attraction for the peninsula. These are three important peninsulas in North America.

There is also an important isthmus you should know in North America. The Isthmus of Panama connects North and South America. It is one of the two most important land bridges in the world. (The other is the Isthmus of Suez, which connects Africa and Asia.)

There are four archipelagoes and three islands you should be able to find on the map. The archipelagoes are the Bahamas and the Antilles in the West Indies. The Bahama Islands are one independent country that is a part of the British Commonwealth. The Antilles Islands are made up of many island nations and territories. The Greater Antilles are the four large islands in the north (top), while the Lesser Antilles are the many smaller islands to the east and south.

The Queen Elizabeth Islands are part of the northern islands, which together are sometimes called the Arctic or Canadian Archipelago. They are so far north that they were not explored until the 1800s. This archipelago of the most northern islands was named after Queen Elizabeth II, who is the ruler of Britain and the official head of the government of Canada.

The <u>Aleutian Islands</u> are a long string of islands stretching out from Alaska toward Asia. They are named after the Aleuts, the Native American people who live there.

The islands you must find on the map are <u>Greenland</u>, <u>Baffin Island</u>, and <u>Newfoundland</u>. Greenland is the world's largest island, and you will learn more about it in the section on countries. Baffin Island is Canada's largest island and the fifth largest in the world. It is named after William Baffin, an English explorer, who visited it in 1616. The island has an arctic climate and few people live there.

Newfoundland (nü' fənd lənd) is an island off the coast of Canada near the mouth of the St. Lawrence River. The **mainland** north of it is called Labrador. The two together are a **province** of Canada. It was here that the Vikings tried to start a colony after traveling from Greenland around the year A.D. 1000. The colony was eventually abandoned and it was not until 1497 that Europeans again set eyes on the "new found land."

| Queen Elizabeth Islands, Canada

| Newfoundland, Canada

| Bahama Islands

Match each item with the correct description.

1.13	_____	Bahamas
1.14	_____	Baja
1.15	_____	Antilles
1.16	_____	Queen Elizabeth
1.17	_____	Yucatan
1.18	_____	Aleutian
1.19	_____	Greenland
1.20	_____	Florida
1.21	_____	Baffin
1.22	_____	Newfoundland
1.23	_____	Panama

a. island string from Alaska toward Asia

b. Mexican peninsula south of California

c. island near the mouth of the St. Lawrence

d. isthmus connecting North and South America

e. British Commonwealth island nation

f. peninsula that divides Caribbean from the Gulf of Mexico

g. world's largest island

h. largest island in Canada

i. archipelago in northern Canada

j. peninsula off the southeast corner of the U.S.

k. West Indies archipelago, divided into Greater and Lesser

The Arctic Ocean is the northern border of North America, while the Atlantic Ocean is the eastern border. Starting in the north (top), there are several parts of the Atlantic Ocean you should know. Between Greenland and Baffin Island is Baffin Bay. Hudson Bay is the huge bay that cuts deep into Canada. It is named after Henry Hudson, the English explorer who mapped the area and died there. The Labrador Sea is the part of the Atlantic between Labrador and the southern end of Greenland.

The Gulf of Mexico is the large gulf between the Florida and Yucatan Peninsulas south of the United States.

The Caribbean Sea is south of the Gulf of Mexico. It is surrounded by Central America, South America, and the Antilles Islands. It is named after the Carib Indians who once lived on the islands.

The Pacific Ocean is the western border of the continent. In the north, the Bering Strait separates Alaska from Russia, and the Bering Sea is the name of the water enclosed by Alaska, Russia, and the Aleutian Islands. The strait and the sea are named after a Danish man who explored the area for Russia. The Gulf of California is the water between the Baja Peninsula and the mainland of Mexico.

| North America

| Sea Lions on the Gulf of California

Each of these features is a part of an ocean. Name the ocean.

1.24 Bering Strait _____

1.25 Hudson Bay _____

1.26 Caribbean Sea _____

1.27 Labrador Sea _____

1.28 Bering Sea _____

1.29 Gulf of California _____

1.30 Gulf of Mexico _____

1.31 Baffin Bay _____

Other Facts

Climate. The climate of North America is tremendously varied. The north is arctic tundra in Alaska and Canada. Much of Central America in the south is tropical rain forest. In between are the middle latitudes, with four seasons that change through the year. There are several desert regions in the Great Basin, much of the southwest United States, and Mexico. Obviously there are many mountains, all with the changes of climate that happen going up in altitude. So, the climate in North America is very different from place to place.

Canada and Greenland (along with Alaska) tend to have colder weather and shorter summers, which means less time to grow crops. The United States is in the middle latitudes, with cool or cold winters and warm or hot summers. It has a great climate for growing crops. Mexico, Central America, and the West Indies have hot, sometimes tropical climates. The desert of Mexico makes it hard to grow crops, while the poor soil of the rain forest makes it difficult to grow food in Central America. The West Indies often have good crop lands, but they are islands and do not have much land to use.

Resources. North America is a continent rich in resources. The Great Plains is one of the best grain-growing areas of the world. The Central Lowlands and the Plains produce wheat, corn, barley, oats, rye, sorghum, cattle, and hogs. Special farms in California,

Texas, and Florida grow many kinds of fruits and vegetables for the people of the United States.

The farms of Canada and the United States are usually large and use modern machines to do the work. Just a few people grow all the food those countries need. In Mexico, the West Indies, and Central America, however, there are many *subsistence farmers*, people who grow just enough to subsist (live). Corn, wheat, and beans are raised to feed the people of Mexico. The larger farms also raise cotton, cattle, sugar, and coffee to sell to other countries.

Much of North America was once covered with vast forests. Huge amounts of the forest land has been cleared for farms, but a great deal remains. Logging is an important industry in Canada and the north-western part of the United States. The trees are used for wood products and to make paper.

North America has huge mineral resources. Canada, the U.S., and Mexico are important producers of petroleum, used to make gasoline. These three major countries also mine many other minerals, such as gold, silver, iron, lead, zinc, and nickel. The United States is a world leader in the production of coal and natural gas. God has richly blessed the continent with the minerals individuals need for manufacturing products.

| Wheat field

| Logging camp

| Coal mining

The **abundance** of resources has allowed the United States and Canada to become two of the wealthiest nations on earth. The harsher climate and problems with their government have stopped Mexico from doing the same. The smaller countries of North America have done well or poorly depending on how well they have used their smaller share of the continent's resources.

Answer *true* or *false*.

1.32 _____ The climate of North America is very much the same all over the continent.

1.33 _____ There are several deserts in North America.

1.34 _____ The United States has the worst climate for growing crops on the continent.

1.35 _____ The wet climate of Mexico makes it hard to grow crops there.

1.36 _____ The Great Plains is a major area for growing coffee and fruit.

1.37 _____ Most of the farms in Canada are large and use modern machines.

1.38 _____ Mexico has many farmers that only grow enough to feed themselves.

1.39 _____ North America's resources include large forests and many minerals.

People. The first settlers to reach North America came from Asia. They crossed from Russia into Alaska thousands of years ago. Many geographers believe there once was a bridge of land, an isthmus, across the Bering Strait. The Asian people used that bridge to **migrate** to North America. Over the years they spread out all over the continent. They formed many different groups or tribes. These tribes learned to live on the new continent and use its resources. We call them Native Americans or Indians.

Greenland was the first part of North America settled by Europeans. Vikings set up a colony there that eventually mixed with the Inuit Native Americans. The Vikings also tried without success to settle in Newfoundland. It was not until the Age of Exploration, however, that Europeans really learned about the continent and began to settle there.

The Europeans, with their more advanced methods of farming, manufacturing, better weapons, and many people, quickly **overwhelmed** the earlier Asian settlers. Because of this, Europe is the **source** of most of the people and culture of North America.

The people of Greenland are a mix of Inuit and Viking blood. Their language and culture is mainly Inuit. Their island was claimed by Denmark, which sent missionaries there in 1721. It is still part of Denmark, but has its own separate government.

Canada was settled by French and British people. Today people of English and French blood are the two largest groups in Canada. Most of the rest are from other European countries. The United States was settled at first by people from Britain, and later settlers accepted the English way of life there. But the U.S. has more groups of people than Canada. English or Irish is the largest group, and German is the second largest. The next two groups are African and Hispanic (people from Spanish-speaking countries). Most of the rest came from other European countries, and a small group is from Asia.

Both Canada and the U.S. were British colonies, and English is still their major language (although French is an important language in Canada). Both countries have systems of

| North Americans are diverse in backgrounds.

democratic government that they learned from Britain. Many people have come to live in both countries from all over the world, but both have a culture that comes from their British **heritage** with a little bit of the rest of Europe added for flavor.

Mexico and Central America were Spanish colonies. The people there are a mix of the original Indians and Spanish. Fewer European people came to those countries than came to the northern countries. Thus, the people today are not so European as they are in Canada and the United States. Their culture includes many Indian ways, as well as European. The most important language is Spanish, however, and Spanish culture is seen everywhere. Thus, the people of the mainland of North America owe most of their heritage to Europe and, in a smaller way, to Asia.

The West Indies are a different story. These islands were claimed by many different nations. Spain, Britain, France, and the Netherlands all had colonies in the West Indies. The Europeans brought in many black African slaves to work the farms they built on the islands. The slaves were eventually given their freedom and became an important part of the people and culture of the islands. The people of the islands today are mainly a mix of African and European. Their culture is a mix of the two continents as well, called *Creole*.

Match each item with the correct culture and people. An item may be used more than once.

1.40	_____ first settlers	a.	African and European; Creole
1.41	_____ Greenland	b.	Asians from Russia
1.42	_____ Canada	c.	largest groups: British, German, African, Hispanic
1.43	_____ United States		
1.44	_____ Mexico	d.	mix of Indian and Spanish
1.45	_____ Central America	e.	mix of Inuit and Viking
1.46	_____ West Indies	f.	mainly British and French

Review the material in this section to prepare for the Self Test. The Self Test will check your understanding of this section. Any items you miss on this test will show you what areas you will need to restudy in order to prepare for the unit test.

SELF TEST 1

Choose the correct letter from the map for each feature (3 points each answer).

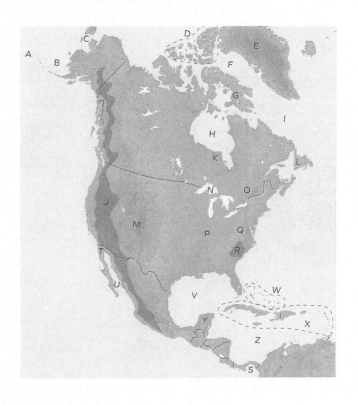

Parts of the ocean

1.01	_____	Labrador Sea
1.02	_____	Bering Sea
1.03	_____	Gulf of Mexico
1.04	_____	Caribbean Sea
1.05	_____	Hudson Bay
1.06	_____	Gulf of California
1.07	_____	Bering Strait
1.08	_____	Baffin Bay

Isthmus

1.09	_____	Panama

Archipelagoes

1.010	_____	Antilles
1.011	_____	Aleutian
1.012	_____	Bahamas
1.013	_____	Queen Elizabeth

Land

1.014	_____	Cordillera
1.015	_____	Appalachian Mtns.
1.016	_____	Great Plains
1.017	_____	Canadian Shield
1.018	_____	Coastal Plains

Waters

1.019	_____	St. Lawrence River
1.020	_____	Mississippi River
1.021	_____	Great Lakes

Peninsulas

1.022	_____	Baja California
1.023	_____	Yucatan

Islands

1.024	_____	Greenland
1.025	_____	Newfoundland
1.026	_____	Baffin

Choose the best word to complete each sentence from the list below (2 points each answer).

Sierra Madre	Great Basin	Rocky	Canada	Greenland
Laurentian	United States	Mexico	West Indies	

1.027 The desert in the center of the mountains of the cordillera in the United States is called the _____ .

1.028 The people of _____ are a mix of Inuit and Viking.

1.029 The people of _____ are a mix of Spanish and Indian.

1.030 _____ is a country that has the Central Lowlands, the Great Plains, and the Coastal Plains for good farmland.

1.031 Many of the people of _____ came from France and Britain.

1.032 The _____ Mountains are part of the cordillera in Mexico.

1.033 The _____ Mountains are the most famous part of the cordillera in the United States.

1.034 The people of _____ are a mix of African and several European countries.

1.035 The _____ Mountains are in Canada along the east (Atlantic) coast.

Answer *true* or *false* (1 point each answer).

1.036 _____ The Great Plains is one of the best areas in the world for growing grain.

1.037 _____ Almost all of the mineral resources in North America are in the United States.

1.038 _____ North America does not have and never did have many forests.

1.039 _____ The first settlers in North America came from Asia and became the many Native American tribes.

Teacher check:

Score _____

Initials _____

Date _____

80 / 100

2. NORTHERN COUNTRIES

The three northern countries in North America are <u>Greenland</u>, <u>Canada</u>, and the <u>United States</u>. In this section you will learn a little about those countries and their history. You will also learn all the states and capitals in the United States. There is a separate states and capitals test for this section.

Objectives

Review these objectives. When you have completed this section, you should be able to:

1. Name and find on a map many of the geographic features of North America.
2. Name the major countries/regions of North America.
3. Name the states on a blank map of the United States.
4. Match U.S. states and their capitals.
5. Tell about the geography, history, and people of the major countries/regions of North America.

Vocabulary

Study these new words. Learning the meanings of these words is a good study habit and will improve your understanding of this LIFEPAC.

butte (byüt). A steep hill that has a flat top and stands alone. A butte is usually smaller than a mesa and not as steep.

communist (kom' yə nist). Countries that believe in a system in which most or all property is owned by the state and is shared by all. The system was set up and kept by force during the Cold War.

contiguous (kən tig' yü əs). Being in actual contact; touching along a boundary or at a point.

continental divide (kon' tə nen' təl di vīd'). A divide separating streams that flow to opposite sides of a continent.

fault (fôlt). A break in the earth's crust, with the mass of rock on one side of the break pushed up, down, or sideways.

federation (fed ə rā' shən). A union by agreement.

horizon (hə rī' zən). The line where earth and sky seem to meet.

megalopolis (meg ə läp'ə ləs). A very large city.

mesa (mā' sə). A high, steep hill that has a flat top and stands alone.

Northwest Passage (nôrth' west' pas' ij). A waterway around mainland North America through the northwest part of the continent.

occupy (ok' yə pī). To take possession of, as by conquest.

survey (sər vā'). To measure for size, shape, position, or boundaries.

uninhabited (un' in hab' ə təd). Not lived in; without people who live there.

Pronunciation Key: hat, āge, cãre, fär; let, ēqual, tėrm; it, īce; hot, ōpen, ôrder; oil; out; cup, pu̇t, rüle; child; long; thin; /ϮH/ for then; /zh/ for measure; /u/ or /ə/ represents /a/ in about, /e/ in taken, /i/ in pencil, /o/ in lemon, and /u/ in circus.

Greenland

| Flag of Greenland

The island of Greenland is also a country. It is a part of Denmark, but makes its own laws. The people are citizens of Denmark, and Denmark takes care of problems with other countries, such as trade matters and treaties, but things like crimes, road building, police, and taxes are handled by Greenland's own government. They also send a representative to the government in Denmark.

Geography. Greenland is the largest island on earth. It is about the same size as the part of the United States that is east of the Mississippi River. Most of the island is covered with a huge, thick cap of ice. Mountains around the edge hold the ice as would the edges of a bowl. Some of it escapes through the valleys to break off and send icebergs into the nearby oceans. Only the land right along the coast is free of ice, and that is where all the people live.

The island is in the Atlantic Ocean, and most of it is inside the Arctic Circle. Baffin Bay and the Davis Strait separate it from Canada. The Denmark Strait separates it from Iceland. Cape Morris Jesup, on the north coast of the island, is the most northern piece of land on earth. No other land is closer to the North Pole.

History. The first people to settle in Greenland were the Inuit. The Inuit are a group of Asian settlers who came to North America later than other Indian groups, but before the Europeans. They spread out all over northeast Asia, Alaska, northern Canada, and Greenland. They were called Eskimos by other Indians. The name Inuit means "the real people" and is usually the name they prefer.

Around the year A.D. 981, a Viking named Eric the Red was forced to leave Iceland for killing someone. He sailed west and discovered the island of Greenland. He explored it, started a settlement there, and named it Greenland in the hopes of attracting settlers from Iceland. The Viking settlement there lost contact with Europe and disappeared by about 1500.

| Greenland (Kaallit Nunaat) and neighboring countries

When Europeans rediscovered the island in their search for the **Northwest Passage**, they found Inuit people there, not Vikings. But some of the Inuit people had blue eyes and blond hair! Inuits from Asia have only dark hair and eyes. Obviously, the blood of the Vikings and the Inuit had mixed.

Denmark sent a missionary named Hans Egede to Greenland in 1721. He established a settlement, taught the people about Jesus, and taught them to read and write. In time, Denmark claimed the whole island. During World War II, while Denmark was **occupied** by the Germans, the United States temporarily controlled the island.

Today. Very few people live in Greenland. The total population in 2015 was about 57,000. That many people often live in a few city blocks of Chicago or Los Angeles. Most of the people live by fishing, hunting

| Colorful houses in Greenland

seals, or trapping fur animals. A few people raise sheep, goats, or cattle on the little bit of ice-free land. The tiny bit of arable land grows only a few kinds of strong plants that are able to grow in the cool, short summers.

Many of the weather changes in the northern hemisphere come from Greenland, so the weather there is carefully watched by countries that travel the northern oceans. The United

| Arch iceberg in Greenland

States has an air base near Thule that watches the weather as well as provides for the protection of the country. The airport there is also important for exploration, because it is so close to the North Pole.

Officially, the people of Greenland use their own Inuit names for their land now. Thus, the capital which was called *Godthab* by the Danes is now *Nuuk*. The name of the island itself officially is *Kalaallit Nunaat*. However, the island will probably always be known as Greenland to the rest of the world.

Match each item with the correct culture and people. An item may be used more than once.

2.1 _____ Davis Strait

2.2 _____ Denmark Strait

2.3 _____ Cape Morris Jesup

2.4 _____ Inuit

2.5 _____ Kalaallit Nunaat

2.6 _____ Nuuk

a. northernmost piece of land on earth

b. first settlers in Greenland

c. water between Greenland and Canada

d. water between Greenland and Iceland

e. official Inuit name for Greenland

f. capital of Greenland

Put the correct word in the blank to complete the sentence.

2.7 The Viking who discovered Greenland and started a settlement there was named _____ .

2.8 _____ was the Danish missionary who came to Greenland in 1721.

2.9 The United States has an airbase in Greenland near the town of _____ .

2.10 The center of Greenland is covered with a huge cap of _____ .

2.11 Greenland is a part of the European country of _____ .

Canada

Canada is a union of ten provinces and three territories. The provinces are very much like states in the United States. Each province has its own government which takes care of education, police, roads, and many other important jobs. The national, or federal, government has important powers to run the whole country.

| Flag of Canada

That is what a "federal" system of government is: states or provinces that have come together and created another government to join them as one nation. Both Canada and the United States have a federal system of government.

Geography. Canada is the largest country in North America and the second largest in the world (only Russia is bigger). The Canadian Shield, the area of rock in northern Canada, is rich in both minerals and lakes. Two of the largest are Great Bear Lake and Great Slave Lake in the Northwest Territories. Canada also claims part of the Great Lakes along the border with the U.S. In all, Canada has more lakes and inland water than any other country in the world!

Canada has large forests for lumber and many beautiful wild places for tourists. The many rivers of the Canadian Shield can be used for hydroelectric power. In fact,

Canada sells electricity to the United States. The prairie provinces of Alberta, Saskatchewan, and Manitoba have rich soil for farming and growing livestock. Canada also has all kinds of metals, natural gas, and oil. Thus, it is a country rich in resources.

| Hydroelectric power plant in Alberta, Canada

The U.S. is Canada's southern border and the state of Alaska touches Canada in the northwest. The United States and Canada share the longest unguarded border in the world. The two countries have been friends for many years and trust each other. Canada's other borders are the Pacific Ocean to the west, the Atlantic Ocean to the east, and the Arctic Ocean to the north.

Canada has three territories that are not provinces. These have too few people to make a province, so the federal government controls the land and natural resources. The people who live there do elect their leaders, but power is given by the federal government. The Yukon and the Northwest Territories have been around for years. However, on April 1, 1999, a new territory in Canada was formed. The eastern part of the Northwest Territories was divided into a new territory called Nunavut. It is governed by the Inuit.

| Dog sled team in Nunavut, Canada

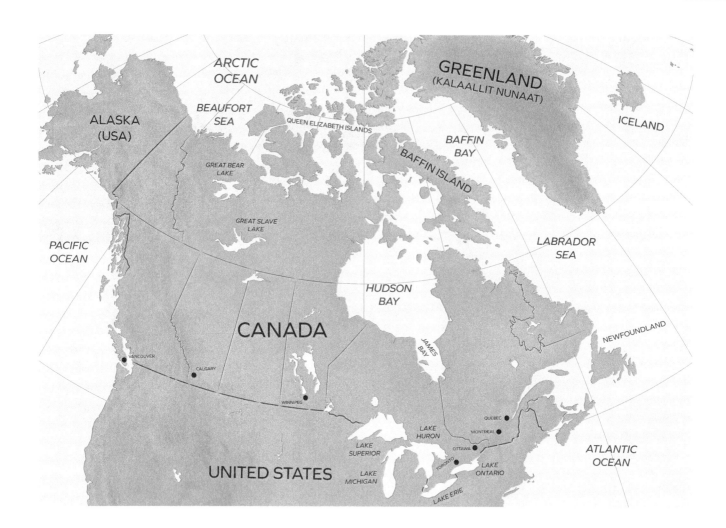

    Map work.

2.12   Using an atlas, encyclopedia, or online resources, put the names of the provinces and territories of Canada on the map. (You need to know the names, but not the locations, for the test.)

2.13   What is the name of the small bay at the southern end of Hudson Bay?

_____

2.14   Which lake is the farthest north, Great Bear or Great Slave?

_____

2.15   What lake is Toronto on? _____

Put the correct word in the blank to complete the sentence.

2.16   Canada has _____ provinces and three territories.

2.17   Both Canada and the United States have a _____ system of government.

2.18   Canada is the _____ largest country in the world.

2.19   Farming is important in the prairie provinces of _____ , _____ , and _____ .

2.20   Two large lakes in the Northwest Territories are _____ and the _____ .

2.21   The ocean north of Canada is the _____ , and the ocean to the east is the _____ .

2.22   In 1999 Canada gained a new territory called _____ , which is run by the _____ people.

History. Canada was inhabited by both Indians and Inuit people at the time of the Age of Exploration. The Vikings had tried to colonize Newfoundland, but failed in about 1000. In 1534 a French explorer by the name of Jacques Cartier traveled up the St. Lawrence River, claiming the land for France. He made three trips to the region for his European homeland.

| Trading fur with Indians

Another Frenchman, Samuel de Champlain, built the first successful settlements in "New France," including the city of Quebec in the early 1600s. These first colonists were interested mostly in the fur trade. Canada had a wealth of beavers, whose fur was wanted in Europe for making hats. France set up a very strict and undemocratic government for the colony.

Britain was setting up colonies in the United States during the time New France was being settled. France and Britain were enemies at the time. It was no surprise when the two countries began fighting over control of North America. From the end of the 1600s to the middle of the 1700s, France and England fought four different wars in North America and Europe. After the last of the wars (known in North America as the French and Indian War), in 1763, New France became a British colony.

Many English-speaking colonists came to the colony in the years that followed. Some were Loyalists who fled from the United States when that country rebelled against England. Many others were immigrants from Britain and Ireland. The French citizens were given special protection for their language and customs under British rule, so Canada developed with both a French and an English way of life.

Several colonies, like Nova Scotia, New Brunswick, and Ontario, were formed from the northern British lands. The colonists there wanted more freedom, just as the American colonists had in 1776. But the Canadian colonies never fought a war against Britain. Instead, they were slowly given more and more freedom by Britain through the 1800s.

Finally, in 1867 four of the colonies joined together to form the Dominion of Canada. Ontario, Quebec, Nova Scotia, and New Brunswick were the first four provinces of the new **federation**. They had their own government, but still accepted the authority of the ruler of Britain. They established their capital in Ontario, in the city of Ottawa. The new government expanded until it controlled all the British land in the north.

| Canadian Parliament in Ottawa, Ontario

Canada fought on the British side in World Wars I and II. After World War II, the United States and Canada worked together to protect themselves against **communist** nations during the Cold War (1945-1989). Canada became a rich manufacturing nation during those years.

Today. Canada is an independent nation in the British Commonwealth. Queen Elizabeth II is the official ruler of the country, but the Prime Minister, who is elected by the Canadian people, actually runs the government.

Canada is not a crowded country. All of the provinces (except Prince Edward Island) have large parts that are **uninhabited**. Most of the people live in the south, near the border with the United States. They live very much like people in the United States, except both French and English are official languages there.

More than half the people are descendants of French or British settlers. The rest are from other European nations, Asia, and Native Americans.

| French and English stop sign in Quebec

The French people have kept their own language and laws, especially in Quebec, which is mainly French. This has caused problems, because the French people are afraid the English-speaking Canadians will push out the French culture. The government of Quebec allows only French to be used for signs and government work in Quebec. The province has voted on leaving the federation to become its own country, but not enough people voted to do it.

The United States, Canada, and Mexico signed an agreement to create a *free-trade zone* between their countries beginning in 1994. The North American Free Trade Agreement (NAFTA) will eventually allow people to trade anywhere in those three countries without paying taxes for goods to cross the border. For the United States and Canada, NAFTA just means continuing to be good neighbors.

| A truck entering the USA

Answer *true* or *false*.

2.23 _____ The French were the first Europeans to land in Canada.

2.24 _____ Jacques Cartier explored Canada for France.

2.25 _____ The first successful French settlements in Canada were begun by Samuel de Champlain.

2.26 _____ The first colonists of New France were interested in the fur trade.

2.27 _____ France and Britain fought several wars in North America.

2.28 _____ Canada developed both an English and Spanish way of life.

2.29 _____ Canada fought its own war for independence from Britain in the 1860s.

2.30 _____ Canada no longer has any government connections with Britain.

2.31 _____ The country of Canada is very crowded, with people spread evenly all over the country.

2.32 _____ The province of Quebec is largely French and afraid of losing their culture in mostly English-speaking Canada.

2.33 _____ NAFTA is a free trade agreement between Canada, the United States, and Mexico.

| Map of Canada

United States

The United States of America is in the center section of North America. It is one of the richest and certainly the most powerful nations on earth. The forty-eight states in the center of the continent are called the **contiguous** states. Two other states, Alaska (northwest of Canada) and Hawaii (in the middle of the Pacific Ocean), are also a part of this nation.

| Flag of the United States

The people of the United States (also called America) came mostly from Europe, seeking both freedom and better lives. They were the type of people who were willing to take a chance on the unknown. They were bold risk-takers. They made the country a "melting pot," where the many cultures of Europe were melted together to create a new culture. These adventurous Americans also worked hard to turn a rich wilderness into farms, cities, and prosperous businesses.

Today America is an English-speaking nation. Most of the people there have ancestors from many different countries. The culture of the country honors hard work and independence. It used to also honor God, but power and pride have made many Americans forget the God who created the land for them.

You will study the history and people of the United States another time. In this LIFEPAC you will learn the states, their capitals, and a little about the geography of the country. You will learn the states in eight sections: Northeast, Southern, Central, Prairie, Mountain, and Pacific states. Each section will begin with a map on which you must put the name of the states as well as the name and location of their capitals.

At the end of this section you will take a special test before you take the Self Test. You will be given a blank map of the United States. You will have to name each state and its capital.

Listed on the next page are the names of the states and their capitals. Use this list and a blank map of the United States to prepare for the special test. You need to be able to find each state on the map and name its capital. (You will not need to locate the capital on a map for the test.)

STATE	CAPITAL	STATE	CAPITAL
ALABAMA	Montgomery	MONTANA	Helena
ALASKA	Juneau	NEBRASKA	Lincoln
ARIZONA	Phoenix	NEVADA	Carson City
ARKANSAS	Little Rock	NEW HAMPSHIRE	Concord
CALIFORNIA	Sacramento	NEW JERSEY	Trenton
COLORADO	Denver	NEW MEXICO	Santa Fe
CONNECTICUT	Hartford	NEW YORK	Albany
DELAWARE	Dover	NORTH CAROLINA	Raleigh
FLORIDA	Tallahassee	NORTH DAKOTA	Bismarck
GEORGIA	Atlanta	OHIO	Columbus
HAWAII	Honolulu	OKLAHOMA	Oklahoma City
IDAHO	Boise	OREGON	Salem
ILLINOIS	Springfield	PENNSYLVANIA	Harrisburg
INDIANA	Indianapolis	RHODE ISLAND	Providence
IOWA	Des Moines	SOUTH CAROLINA	Columbia
KANSAS	Topeka	SOUTH DAKOTA	Pierre
KENTUCKY	Frankfort	TENNESSEE	Nashville
LOUISIANA	Baton Rouge	TEXAS	Austin
MAINE	Augusta	UTAH	Salt Lake City
MARYLAND	Annapolis	VERMONT	Montpelier
MASSACHUSETTS	Boston	VIRGINIA	Richmond
MICHIGAN	Lansing	WASHINGTON	Olympia
MINNESOTA	St. Paul	WEST VIRGINIA	Charleston
MISSISSIPPI	Jackson	WISCONSIN	Madison
MISSOURI	Jefferson City	WYOMING	Cheyenne

2.34 Using an atlas, encyclopedia, or online resources, label each Northeast state. Put a dot on the map where each state capital is located and label it.

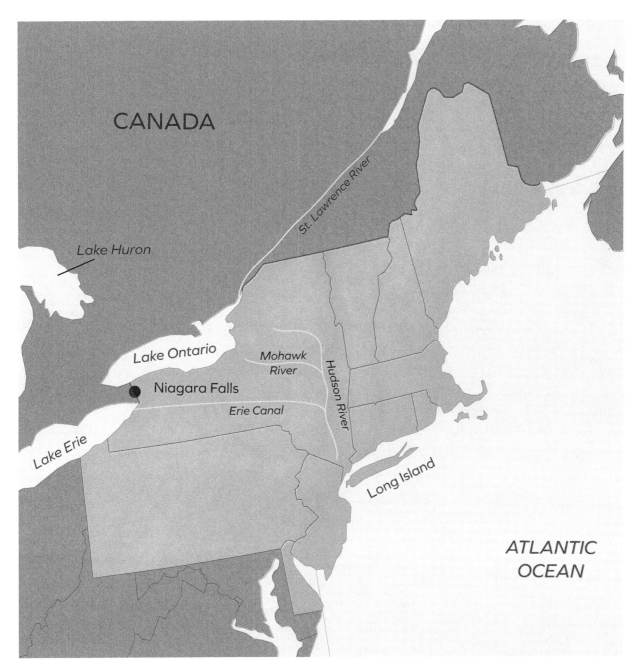

CANADA

St. Lawrence River

Lake Huron

Lake Ontario

Mohawk River

Hudson River

Niagara Falls

Erie Canal

Lake Erie

Long Island

ATLANTIC OCEAN

| Northeast States

Teacher check:

Initials _____ Date _____

The Northeast is where the second American colony founded by the British began. The settlers came to Plymouth, Massachusetts in 1620. They were Christians who were escaping persecution in England by the state church. We call them the Pilgrims.

The colonists naturally named the land "New England" after their home. That name is still used for the states of Maine, Vermont, New Hampshire, Massachusetts, Connecticut, and Rhode Island. It became a land of small farms and close-knit towns. The deep religious faith of the people created a stable, hard-working group.

| Pilgrim settlers in Plymouth, Massachusetts

The land of New England is mostly mountains, the Appalachian Mountains. The Green, White, and Blue Mountains are the best-known ranges in the area. The thin strip of the Coastal Plains is the best land. The soil is usually thin and rocky. But, there is plenty of water and with hard work, the farmers grew enough to survive.

The Northeast is a beautiful section of the country. The mountains and hills are covered with forests. They glimmer with a white blanket of snow in the winter and a deep green covering in the summer. In the fall the hills are covered with bright trees dancing in their changing colors. The mountains, forests, and streams are a delight to people who love the outdoors.

Eventually, the fast-moving streams that tumbled down out of the mountains were put to practical use. They were used to power machines to spin thread, weave cloth, and make other goods. America's first factories began in the Northeast in the 1700-1800s. For many years it was the main manufacturing center of the country. Gradually, however, other places have replaced it. Today much of the Northeast's industry is too old and has been shut down.

The Northeast, along with Virginia from the South, was the heartland of the country when the United States was formed in 1776. Virginia was the first and largest colony. New York City and Philadelphia, Pennsylvania were the largest cities. Much of the Revolutionary War, which won freedom from Britain, was fought in these states.

The Catskill and Adirondack Ranges are part of the Appalachians in New York. The mountains run through most of the Northeast states, but the Coastal Plains get wider south of New England, providing more good farmland. Also, the Hudson and Mohawk Rivers cut through the mountains in New York. This creates a fertile valley, as well as a way to cross the highlands. In 1825, the Erie Canal connected the Mohawk River with Lake Erie. That meant that goods could be shipped from the Great Lakes through the canal and rivers to New York City on the Atlantic Ocean.

The Northeast port cities of Boston, Philadelphia, Baltimore, and New York grew huge on the trade between America and the world. They also grew bigger as industries were built all over the Northeast in the 1800s. Today these are **megalopolises** that spread for miles along the coast.

There are many important features in these states. Niagara Falls is on the river between Lake Erie and Ontario in New York. The St. Lawrence River forms part of the border between New York and Canada. Also off the coast of New York is Long Island, the largest island in the contiguous states. The Atlantic coastline is dotted with sand beaches and has many barrier islands. The Allegheny and Monongahela Rivers, on the western side of the mountains, meet at Pittsburgh, Pennsylvania. They join to create the Ohio River, which drains west into the great Mississippi River.

| The Erie Canal

Choose the correct letter to match these items.

2.35	_____	Pilgrims
2.36	_____	Catskill
2.37	_____	Erie
2.38	_____	Ohio
2.39	_____	Niagara
2.40	_____	New England
2.41	_____	Hudson
2.42	_____	St. Lawrence

a. waterfall between Lakes Erie and Ontario

b. Monongahela and Allegheny Rivers make this river when they meet at Pittsburgh

c. Maine, Vermont, New Hampshire, Massachusetts, Connecticut, Rhode Island

d. mountain range in the Appalachians

e. river that cuts through the mountains in New York

f. canal that connected Lake Erie and the Mohawk River

g. river between New York and Canada

h. settled at Plymouth, Massachusetts in 1620

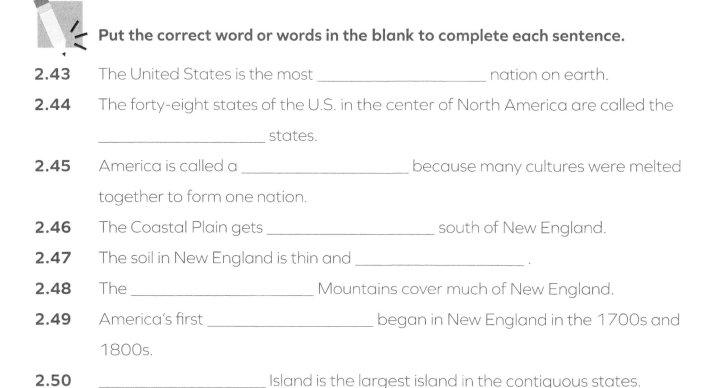

Put the correct word or words in the blank to complete each sentence.

2.43 The United States is the most _____ nation on earth.

2.44 The forty-eight states of the U.S. in the center of North America are called the _____ states.

2.45 America is called a _____ because many cultures were melted together to form one nation.

2.46 The Coastal Plain gets _____ south of New England.

2.47 The soil in New England is thin and _____ .

2.48 The _____ Mountains cover much of New England.

2.49 America's first _____ began in New England in the 1700s and 1800s.

2.50 _____ Island is the largest island in the contiguous states.

HISTORY & GEOGRAPHY 409

LIFEPAC TEST

NAME _____

DATE _____

SCORE _____

HISTORY & GEOGRAPHY 409: LIFEPAC TEST

Choose the letter that best matches each feature. Each letter is used only once (3 points each answer).

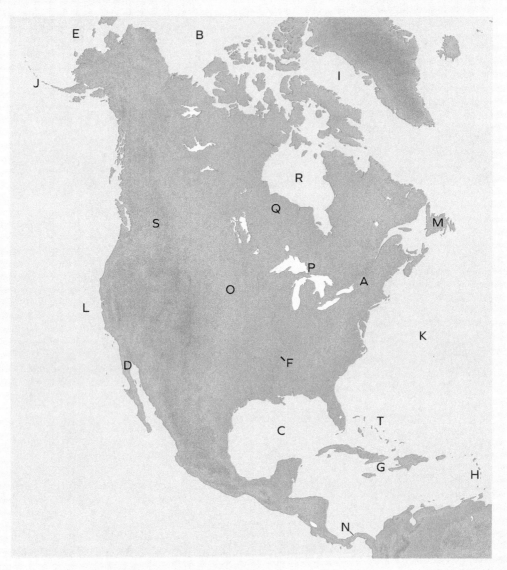

1. _____	Mississippi River	2. _____	Isthmus of Panama
3. _____	Aleutian Archipelago	4. _____	Arctic Ocean
5. _____	Baja California	6. _____	Bahama Archipelago
7. _____	Cordillera	8. _____	Atlantic Ocean
9. _____	Pacific Ocean	10. _____	Hudson Bay

11. _____ Great Lakes
12. _____ Greater Antilles
13. _____ Lesser Antilles
14. _____ Baffin Bay
15. _____ Gulf of Mexico
16. _____ Canadian Shield
17. _____ Bering Sea
18. _____ Great Plains
19. _____ St. Lawrence River
20. _____ Newfoundland

Match these items (2 points each answer).

21. _____ Maya
22. _____ Great Basin
23. _____ Costa Rica, Belize
24. _____ Saskatchewan, Quebec
25. _____ Greenland
26. _____ Superior
27. _____ District of Columbia
28. _____ Sierra Madre
29. _____ Canada
30. _____ Appalachian

a. Central American countries
b. world's largest lake
c. location of U.S. capital
d. mountains in eastern America
e. cordillera in Mexico
f. North America's largest country
g. provinces of Canada
h. civilization in Mexico and central America before Columbus
i. world's largest island
j. desert in the American cordillera

Answer *true* or *false* (1 point each answer).

31. _____ Mexico is a central plateau surrounded by mountains and narrow coastal plains.

32. _____ The Canadian Shield has many lakes, rivers, and minerals.

33. _____ The Mason-Dixon Line divides the north and the south in American history.

34. _____ Most of Greenland is covered by an ice cap.

35. _____ The people of the West Indies are a mixture of African and many European countries.

36. _____ The people of Mexico are a mixture of Spanish and Native American.

37. _____ Greenland was the first place in North America that Columbus discovered.

38. _____ The Great Plains is a desert that is very poor for farmland.

39. _____ The Piedmont Plateau is between the Appalachian Mountains and the Coastal Plains in the U.S.

40. _____ Mexico has very few mineral resources.

41. _____ The very first settlers in North America came from Asia through Alaska.

42. _____ Puerto Rico, the Windward Islands, and Hispaniola are part of the Queen Elizabeth Islands.

43. _____ The people of Greenland are a mixture of Inuit and Spanish.

44. _____ The West Indies are all flat, coral islands.

45. _____ The cordillera goes from Alaska to Central America.

46. _____ North America is connected to Europe by the Baffin Strait.

47. _____ Most of the countries of Central America were Spanish colonies.

48. _____ There are no rain forests or tundras in North America.

49. _____ The Mississippi River has tributaries that begin in both the cordillera and the Appalachians.

50. _____ The Bahamas and Canada are part of the British Commonwealth.

2.51   Using an atlas, encyclopedia, or online resources, label each Southern state. Put a dot on the map where each state capital is located and label it.

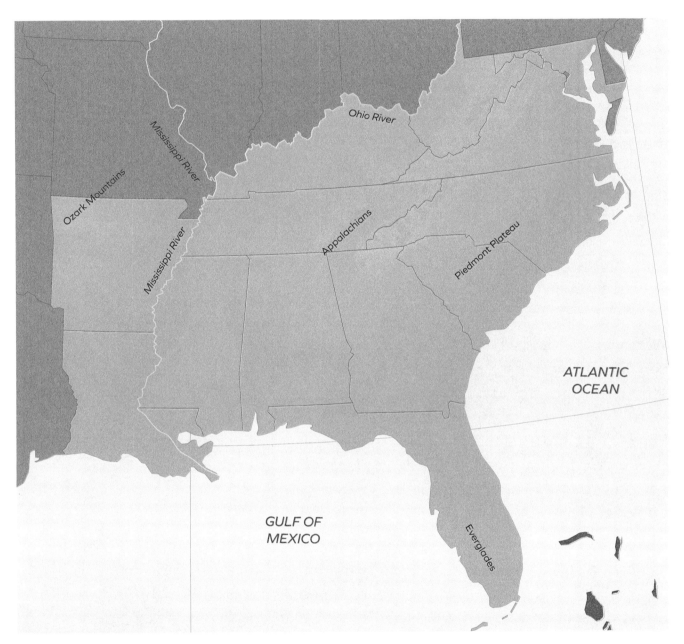

| Southern States

Teacher check:

Initials _____   Date _____

The Southern states begin south of Pennsylvania at the Mason-Dixon Line. The Mason-Dixon Line began as the border between Maryland and Pennsylvania. It is named after the two men who **surveyed** and set it in the 1760s. Over many years people began to think of it as the line which separated the North from the South in American history. It included not only the border of Maryland, but the northern border of the states that allowed blacks to be kept as slaves in the mid-1800s. The Mason-Dixon Line, therefore, also ran along the Ohio River, the northern border of both West Virginia and Kentucky.

It was the Southern states that formed most of the Confederate States of America in 1860 at the start of the Civil War. Those states wanted to keep slaves to grow their crops, while the Northern states wanted to end slavery. The Southern states tried to rebel and form their own country. After five years of terrible war, they were forced to stay in the United States and free their slaves.

West Virginia had just been part of Virginia before that time, but the people of that area separated from Virginia and created their own state. They did not want to join the Confederacy. Because the capital of the United States, Washington D.C., is in Maryland, U.S. soldiers came into the state and would not let it join the Confederacy.

| Confederate General

The capital of the United States is built on land taken from Maryland and Virginia in 1790. The 10-mile-square piece of land was named the District of Columbia (after Columbus). The capital city built there was named Washington after the first president. Eventually the city got so big it filled the whole District. Today, the capital is called Washington, District of Columbia, or Washington, D.C. for short.

The Coastal Plains that run along the Atlantic and Gulf coast are the biggest land feature of the Southern states. The good farmland and many rivers to transport crops attracted the settlers. The Appalachian Mountains run mainly through West Virginia, Kentucky, and Tennessee. Between the mountains and the plains, however, is another important feature, the Piedmont Plateau.

| The Ozark Mountains

The Piedmont Plateau is a gently rolling plateau between the Coastal Plains and the Appalachian Mountains in the South. It is a part of the Appalachian Highlands. The plateau runs between the plains and the Appalachians all the way from New Jersey to Alabama. The soil is not as good as in the plains, but it is better than in the mountains, and many crops are grown there. The drop from the plateau to the plains can be very steep, and rivers usually form waterfalls there. Many cities have been built on this "fall line" to take advantage of the power from the waterfalls.

There is one other area of highland you need to know in this section. That is the Ozark Mountains. The Ozarks are located where Arkansas, Missouri, and Oklahoma touch. Those three states are in three different sections, so we will mention the Ozarks here. In the United States, it is one of two important highland areas between the Appalachian Mountains and the cordillera.

The Ohio River begins at Pittsburgh, Pennsylvania and forms the northern border of this section of states. It joins the Mississippi River where Illinois, Kentucky, and Missouri meet. From there, the Mississippi goes south to the Gulf of Mexico. The greatest river in

| River boat on the Mississippi River

North America, the Mississippi, has tributaries that come from both the Appalachian Mountains in the east and the cordillera in the west. It is an American river that has a drainage basin that covers the entire center of the contiguous states.

Put the correct word(s) in the blank to complete the sentence.

2.52   The _____ Line divides the North from the South in American history.

2.53   Most of the Southern states were a part of the _____ States of America during the Civil War.

2.54   The state of _____ separated from Virginia at the start of the Civil War.

2.55   The full name of the capital of the United States (no abbreviations) is

_____ .

2.56   The land for the capital was taken from the states of _____ and _____ .

2.57   The biggest land feature of the Southern states is the _____ Plains.

2.58   From New Jersey and Alabama, the _____ Plateau lies between the Appalachians and the plains.

2.59   The _____ Mountains are in the area where Oklahoma, Arkansas, and Missouri meet.

2.60   The _____ River forms the northern border of West Virginia and Kentucky.

2.61   The _____ is the greatest river in the United States and North America.

2.62   Using an atlas, encyclopedia, or online resources, label each Central state.

Put a dot on the map where each state capital is located and label it.

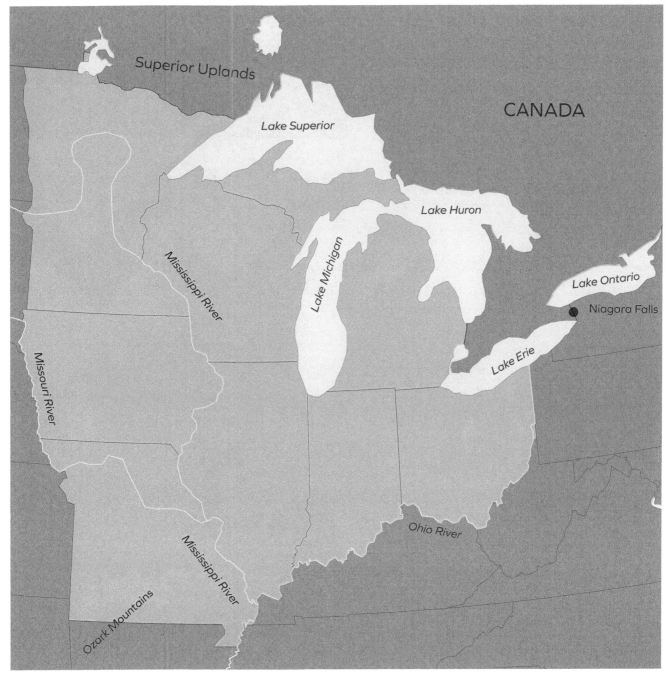

| Central States

Teacher check:

Initials _____ Date _____

The Central states are in the Central Lowlands of North America. There is one small area of higher land in this section. It is called the Superior Uplands. It is the second important area of highlands between the Appalachians and the cordillera (the other was the Ozarks). The Superior Uplands are located at the west (left, on the map) end of Lake Superior, the largest of the Great Lakes (also the largest lake in the world). It is a hilly, rocky area covered with beautiful lakes.

| An ocean-going barge can go from the Atlantic ocean to Detroit, Michigan via the St. Lawrence Seaway.

The Great Lakes form most of the border between the U.S. and Canada in this region. Lake Michigan is the only one of the Great Lakes that is completely in the United States. The other four lakes are half in the U.S. and half in Canada.

All of the Great Lakes are part of the St. Lawrence Seaway. The Seaway uses canals, rivers, and the Great Lakes to provide a way for ocean ships to reach cities far away from the ocean. The result is another coastline for America and Canada. Chicago, Illinois on Lake Michigan is about 700 miles from the Atlantic Ocean, but it is still a port city for ships that sail on the Atlantic!

The Central Lowlands have excellent farmland. The colder temperatures of the most northern states do limit the crops that can be grown there, but the rich, well-watered lands of Iowa, Missouri, Illinois, Indiana, and Ohio produce abundant crops.

The Mississippi River runs through the center of this section. The source of the Mississippi itself is in the Superior Uplands. From its source in Minnesota it flows south to reach the Gulf of Mexico in Louisiana. The Mississippi is a border for many states as it crosses the country. For example, the river forms the entire eastern border for the states of Iowa, Missouri, and Arkansas.

Another important tributary, the Missouri River, joins the Mississippi near St. Louis, Missouri. The source of the Missouri is in the Rocky Mountains of the cordillera. These rivers and the Great Lakes allowed settlers to go deep into this land long before roads could be built. This land, on the far side of the Appalachians, was next to be settled after the east coast.

Answer *true* or *false*.

2.63 _____ The Superior Uplands are a plateau between Lake Superior and Lake Michigan.

2.64 _____ All five of the Great Lakes are half in Canada and half in the U.S.

2.65 _____ The St. Lawrence Seaway allows ships to travel from the Great Lakes down the Mississippi to the Gulf of Mexico.

2.66 _____ Chicago, Illinois is a port city for ocean ships.

2.67 _____ The Central Lowlands have excellent farmland.

2.68 _____ The source of the Missouri River is in the cordillera.

2.69 _____ The source of the Mississippi River is in the Appalachian Mountains.

2.70 _____ The Mississippi River flows into the Caribbean Sea from the state of Mississippi.

2.71 Using an atlas, encyclopedia, or online resources, label each state. Put a dot on the map where each Prairie state capital is located and label it.

Teacher check:

Initials _____

Date _____

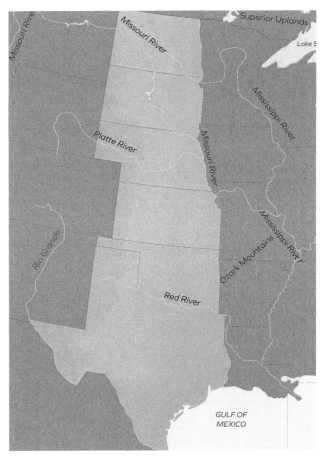

| Prairie States

The Prairie states are on the Great Plains of North America. The land is very flat and slowly slopes upward toward the Rocky Mountains like a tilted table top. The word *prairie* comes from a French word for meadow. Before the coming of the Europeans the Great Plains were a vast meadow, a sea of grass stretching out to the **horizon** in every direction. The land has few trees and was once the home of great herds of wild buffaloes.

The wide open spaces of the Great Plains can make for very difficult weather. Wind and storms come in swiftly, with nothing to block their path. Sudden changes in weather and temperature are normal. Tornadoes or cyclones are very common, especially in Texas, Oklahoma, and Kansas. These are twisting clouds that come down out of thunder storms. When they touch the ground they suck in the things in their path, causing great damage.

The long arms of the Mississippi reach even into this dry place for tributaries. The Missouri River and its tributary, the Platte River, flow through the Dakotas and Nebraska. The Red River that is part of the border between Texas and Oklahoma is also a Mississippi tributary. But the Rio Grande River, which separates Texas from Mexico does not flow into the Mississippi. Instead, it finds its own, independent way to the Gulf of Mexico.

The land of the Great Plains was some of the last settled in the United States. Many of the early explorers thought that people could not live there because it was so dry. In fact, the land does get drier and more desert-like as you get closer to the cordillera and their rain shadow. People headed for new settlements in Oregon and California, beyond the mountains, passed quickly through this supposedly barren desert.

However, much of the prairie land is perfect for growing wheat and grain and raising cattle. It was the cattle ranchers who first tried to settle the land, fattening huge herds of cattle for market. Eventually, however, it was the Homestead Acts that brought in settlers.

| A combine loads grain into a wagon.

After the Civil War (1860-1865), Congress passed laws that gave land to any citizen who lived on it or farmed it for five years. Called the Homestead Acts, these laws brought settlers to the empty prairies. The promise of free land brought people willing to try farming in the harsh climate. Many failed and returned east. Those who succeeded turned the American prairie into the greatest grain-growing area of the world.

Answer *true* or *false*.

2.72 _____ The prairie is part of the Coastal Plains.

2.73 _____ Prairie comes from a French word for meadow.

2.74 _____ Tornadoes are a danger on the Great Plains.

2.75 _____ The Platte River is a tributary of the Missouri.

2.76 _____ The Rio Grande River is a tributary of the Mississippi.

2.77 _____ Prairie land gets a large amount of rain, particularly near the mountains.

2.78 _____ The Homestead Act brought many settlers to the prairie.

2.79 _____ Wheat and grain grow well on much of the Great Plains.

2.80 Using an atlas, encyclopedia, or online resources, label each Mountain state. Put a dot on the map where each state capital is located and label it.

Teacher check:

Initials _____

Date _____

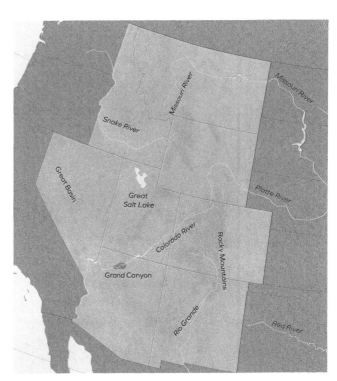

| Mountain States

The Mountain states are right on top of the cordillera. The Rocky Mountains run all along the east side of this section, like a wall beside the floor of the Great Plains.

The first high ridge of the Rocky Mountains coming up from the Great Plains is the **continental divide**. The arms of the Mississippi go no further west. In Colorado, the source of the South Platte River is on the east side of the divide. The Platte will join the Missouri and the Mississippi to flow into the Atlantic at the Gulf of Mexico. On the western side of that same mountain ridge in Colorado is the source of the Colorado River. The Colorado will flow to the Gulf of California in the Pacific.

Because the mountains of the Pacific coast block the moisture from the ocean, this section of America is very dry. Much of it is real desert. The Great Basin Desert, for example, is in Nevada and Utah. It is like a bowl lying between the Rocky Mountains and the Sierra Nevada Mountains of California. The little rain that does fall there does not reach either ocean. Some of it drains into the Great Salt Lake. There it evaporates, leaving salty water behind. The Great Salt Lake is the largest lake west of the Great Lakes and one of the saltiest lakes in the world.

| The Grand Canyon

What this region lacks in green plants, it makes up for in spectacular scenery. The huge mountains, deep canyons, and brilliant-colored rocks attract tourists from all over the world. The excellent skiing also attracts many winter visitors.

The most famous feature of the Mountain states is the Grand Canyon in Arizona. The Grand Canyon is a 277 mile (446 km)-long canyon that is more than 5000 feet (1500 m) deep and 18 miles (29 km) wide in places. The Colorado River flows through the bottom of it. The many colored layers of rock, tall **buttes**, and beautiful **mesas** attract millions of visitors every year.

The Mountain states have very little land that is good for growing crops. Some of the grassland can be used for raising cattle, and crops can be irrigated or grown in river valleys. But for years the biggest attractions for this section were the minerals in the mountains and the beautiful scenery. Today, however, these states are growing rapidly as people move in to find jobs in the many businesses there.

Put the correct word(s) in the blank to complete the sentence.

2.81   The continental divide for the United States is in the _____ Mountains.

2.82   The sources of both the South Platte and Colorado Rivers are in the state of

_____ .

2.83   The _____ Desert is a bowl-shaped desert in Nevada and Utah.

2.84   The largest lake in America west of the Great Lakes is the _____ Lake.

2.85   The _____ Canyon is over 200 miles long on the Colorado River in Arizona.

2.86   Using an atlas, encyclopedia, or online resources, label each Pacific state. Put a dot on the map where each state capital is located and label it.

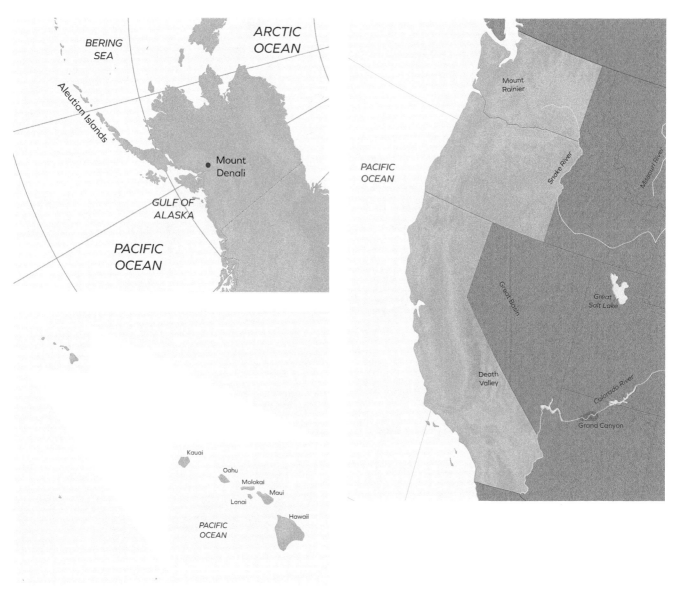

| Pacific States

Teacher check:

Initials _____   Date _____

The Pacific states are all mountainous states on the Pacific Ocean. The cordillera covers California, Oregon, Washington, and Alaska. The Sierra Nevada in California, the Cascades in Washington, and the Brooks Range in Alaska are just some of the mountains of this section. The tallest mountain in the U.S., Denali, is in the Alaska Range of the cordillera. Some of the mountains, called the Coastal Ranges, reach right to the edge of the ocean. The Pacific coast does not have a wide coastal plain like the Atlantic side of the country.

Hawaii, however, is not in the cordillera. It is an archipelago of volcanic islands in the middle of the Pacific Ocean. There are tall volcanic mountains on the big islands. Some of the smaller islands are atolls left when the volcanoes sank back into the sea.

The Pacific states are places where the earth is not predictable. Alaska, Washington, Oregon, and California are all on top of **faults** in the earth, where earthquakes often occur. One such earthquake near San Francisco, California occurred in 1989, killing over 60 people and interrupted the World Series. Another in Alaska in 1964 killed over 130 people.

Volcanoes are another danger in the Pacific states. They can erupt along the faults. Mount Saint Helens in the Cascade Range of Washington erupted in 1980, killing 57 people. Several of the volcanic mountains that formed the Hawaiian Islands are still active. The lava from the volcanoes continues to make the island of Hawaii, the biggest island of the archipelago, bigger by adding land along the edge of the sea. Eruptions and earthquakes sometimes occur together there. Many visitors like to see the lava

| Volcano on Hawaiian island, Kilauea

flowing at Hawaii Volcanoes National Park on the island of Hawaii.

The five Pacific states have many different climates. Parts of Alaska are north of the Arctic Circle, and Arctic tundra covers much of the north end of the state. Hawaii, on the other hand, is a tropical archipelago. Several of the islands have rain forests on the sides of their mountains. California, Washington, and Oregon have wet, mild climates near the ocean (remember oceans tend to keep nearby land warmer in winter and cooler in the summer).

In California, Oregon, and Washington the land gets drier and drier as it moves inland across the rain-blocking mountains. There are several deserts on the east side of the states, including the Mojave Desert and Death Valley in California. Death Valley is the lowest spot of land in the entire Western Hemisphere! It is 282 feet (86 m) below sea level.

Almost all of eastern Oregon is desert, but not eastern Washington. The Columbia River and its tributary, the Snake River, wind through that part of the state, watering the dry, prairie-like land. The Columbia and the Snake form part of the border for the states of Oregon and Washington. The Colorado forms the border of Arizona and California, on one of the last parts of its journey toward the Gulf of California.

Answer *true* or *false*.

2.87 _____ Most of the Pacific states are coastal plains.

2.88 _____ The Sierra Nevada and the Cascades are part of the mountains of the cordillera in the Pacific states.

2.89 _____ The state of Hawaii is an island near the coast of Alaska created by the mountains of the cordillera as they go out into the ocean.

2.90 _____ Earthquakes are a danger in the Pacific states.

2.91 _____ There are no active volcanoes in the Pacific states.

2.92 _____ The Pacific states all have the same climate, wet and warm.

2.93 _____ Death Valley is the lowest spot of land in North America.

2.94 _____ The Columbia and Snake Rivers form part of the borders for the Washington and Oregon.

2.95 _____ The Colorado River flows into the Atlantic Ocean.

Review the material in this section to prepare for the Self Test. The Self Test will check your understanding of this section and will review the other sections. Any items you miss on this test will show you what areas you will need to restudy in order to prepare for the unit test.

Review. Use this map as practice for the states and capitals test.

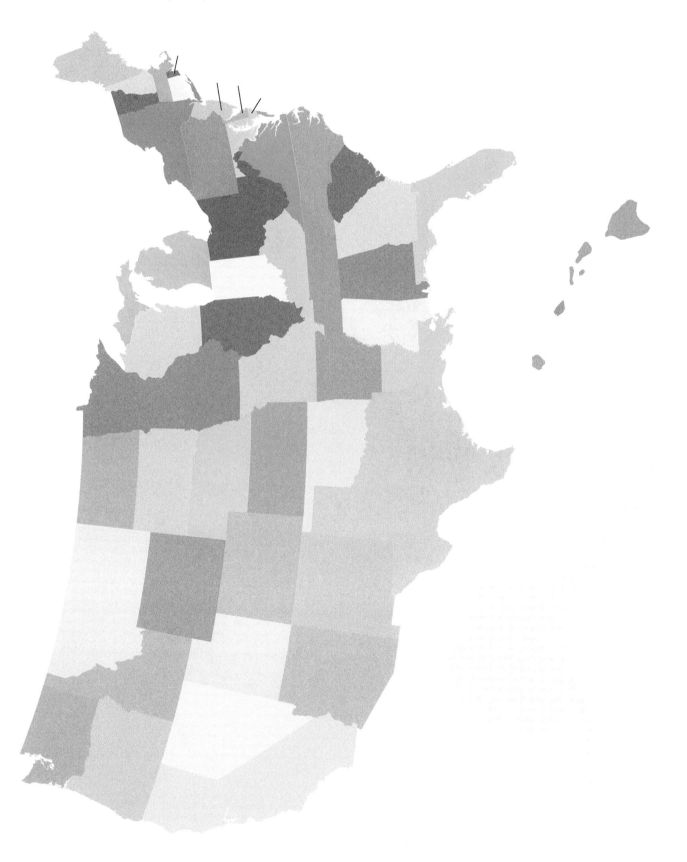

Map for States and Capitals Test

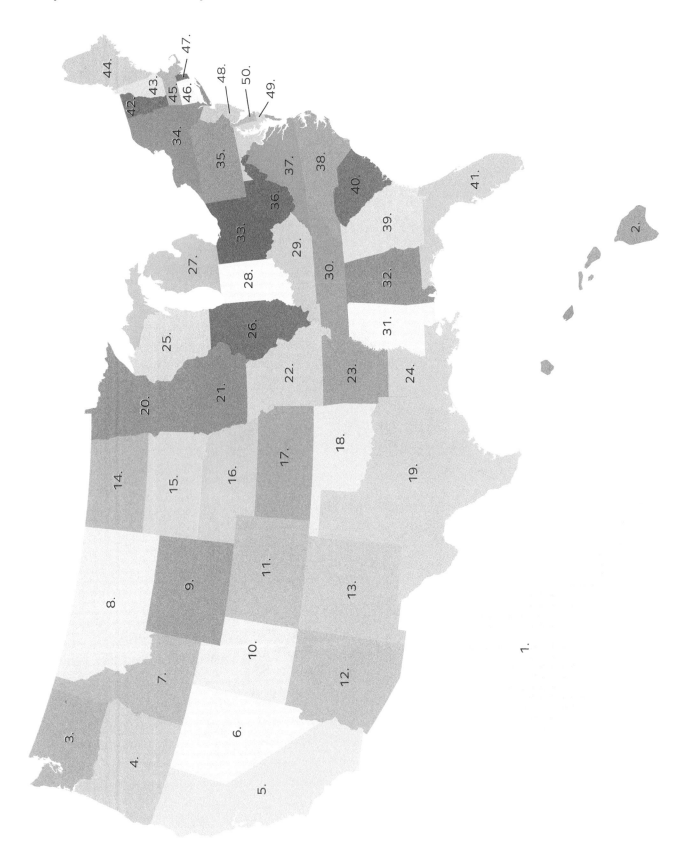

STATES AND CAPITALS TEST

Look at the States and Capitals Test map. Using the numbers on the map, write the correct state and capital on a clean sheet of paper (each state or capital, 1 point). Answers are in the Answer Key.

STATES

Alabama	Alaska	Arizona	Arkansas	California
Colorado	Connecticut	Delaware	Florida	Georgia
Hawaii	Idaho	Illinois	Indiana	Iowa
Kansas	Kentucky	Louisiana	Maine	Maryland
Massachusetts	Michigan	Minnesota	Mississippi	Missouri
Montana	Nebraska	Nevada	New Hampshire	New Jersey
New Mexico	New York	North Carolina	North Dakota	Ohio
Oklahoma	Oregon	Pennsylvania	Rhode Island	South Carolina
South Dakota	Tennessee	Texas	Utah	Vermont
Virginia	Washington	West Virginia	Wisconsin	Wyoming

CAPITALS

Albany	Annapolis	Atlanta	Augusta	Austin
Baton Rouge	Bismarck	Boise	Boston	Carson City
Charleston	Cheyenne	Columbia	Columbus	Concord
Denver	Des Moines	Dover	Frankfort	Harrisburg
Hartford	Helena	Honolulu	Indianapolis	Jackson
Jefferson City	Juneau	Lansing	Lincoln	Little Rock
Madison	Montgomery	Montpelier	Nashville	Oklahoma City
Olympia	Phoenix	Pierre	Providence	Raleigh
Richmond	Sacramento	St. Paul	Salem	Salt Lake City
Santa Fe	Springfield	Tallahassee	Topeka	Trenton

✔ **Teacher check:**   Initials _____

Score _____   Date _____

80 / 100

SELF TEST 2

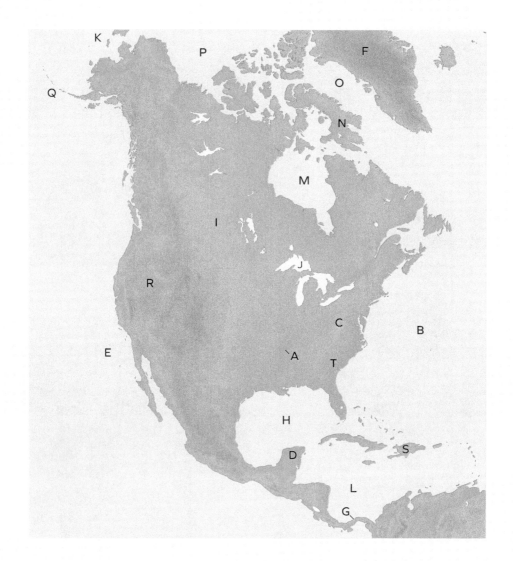

Using the map above, put the correct letter next to the name. Each is used only once (3 points each answer).

2.01 _____ Isthmus of Panama

2.02 _____ Great Plains

2.03 _____ Mississippi River

2.04 _____ Pacific Ocean

2.05 _____ Yucatan Peninsula

2.06 _____ Bering Sea

2.07 _____ Caribbean Sea

2.08 _____ Arctic Ocean

2.09 _____ Hudson Bay

2.010 _____ Aleutian Archipelago

2.011 _____ Baffin Island

2.012 _____ Appalachian Mountains

2.013 _____ Greenland   **2.014** _____ Great Lakes

2.015 _____ Antilles Archipelago   **2.016** _____ Gulf of Mexico

2.017 _____ Atlantic Ocean   **2.018** _____ Coastal Plains

2.019 _____ Baffin Bay   **2.020** _____ Cordillera

Put a _G_ if the statement is true of Greenland, a _C_ if it is true of Canada, and a _U_ if it is true of the United States (2 points each answer).

2.021 _____ the largest island on earth

2.022 _____ largest country in North America

2.023 _____ the mountains include the Rocky, Catskill, Brooks, Sierra Nevada, and White Mountains

2.024 _____ Lake Michigan is there

2.025 _____ was a colony of Denmark

2.026 _____ capital is in the District of Columbia

2.027 _____ forty-eight contiguous states in the center of the continent

2.028 _____ includes the provinces of Nova Scotia, Ontario, and Prince Edward Island

2.029 _____ is a member of the British Commonwealth

2.030 _____ most of it is covered by an ice cap

Match these items (2 points each answer).

2.031	_____	Mason-Dixon Line
2.032	_____	Kalaallit Nunaat
2.033	_____	Cape Morris Jesup
2.034	_____	Great Basin
2.035	_____	Sierra Madre
2.036	_____	Yukon
2.037	_____	Quebec
2.038	_____	Niagara
2.039	_____	St. Lawrence
2.040	_____	Piedmont

a. river that connects the Great Lakes to the Atlantic Ocean

b. mountains of the cordillera in Mexico

c. Inuit name for Greenland

d. territory in Canada

e. waterfall between Lakes Erie and Ontario

f. plateau between the Appalachians and Coastal Plains

g. line between the south and the north in U.S. history

h. most northern point of land on earth

i. mostly French-speaking Canadian province

j. American desert in the cordillera

Teacher check:

Score _____

Initials _____

Date _____

80 / 100

3. SOUTHERN COUNTRIES

The southern countries of North America can be divided into <u>Mexico</u>, <u>Central America</u>, and the <u>West Indies</u>. You will learn about the geography of these areas and something of their history in this section. You will learn the names of the nations in Central America and some of the important island nations of the West Indies. The culture and history of these nations is very different from the northern countries.

Objectives

Review these objectives. When you have completed this section, you should be able to:

1. Name and find on a map many of the geographic features of North America.
2. Name the major countries/regions of North America.
5. Tell about the geography, history, and people of the major countries/regions of North America.
6. Recognize the names of the countries of Central America.
7. Recognize the names of the major islands of the West Indies.

Vocabulary

Study these new words. Learning the meanings of these words is a good study habit and will improve your understanding of this LIFEPAC.

estate (ə stāt′). A large piece of land, usually with a large house on it.

extension (ik sten′ shən). An addition.

turmoil (tėr′ moil). A commotion; disturbance; disorder.

Pronunciation Key: hat, āge, cãre, fär; let, ēqual, tėrm; it, īce; hot, ōpen, ôrder; oil; out; cup, pu̇t, rüle; child; long; thin; /ŦH/ for then; /zh/ for measure; /u/ or /ə/ represents /a/ in about, /e/ in taken, /i/ in pencil, /o/ in lemon, and /u/ in circus.

Mexico

| Flag of Mexico

Mexico is a federal republic like the U.S. and Canada. Its capital is Mexico City, near the center of the southern part of the country. The people of Mexico are mainly a mix of Native Americans and the Spanish who conquered the country. There is still a large part of the population that is Native American (about one out of three), but most of the people are *mestizo*, European and Indian. Their culture is a mix of Spanish and Indian also. Art, music, and buildings all show a blending of the two cultures.

Geography. Most of the country of Mexico is a plateau surrounded by the Sierra Madre Mountains. The Sierra Madre Occidental (West Sierras) are an **extension** of the Sierra Nevada Mountains in the U.S. In the same way, the Sierra Madre Oriental (East Sierras) are an extension of the Rocky Mountains. The Coastal Ranges of the Pacific coast also continue in Mexico on the Baja Peninsula. The Sierra Madre del Sur (South Sierras) sweep along the Pacific coast, connecting the east and west mountains.

The *Central Plateau* is the heartland of Mexico. The climate is dry because of the mountains that surround it. Crops can be grown on the plateau, but they often need irrigation, and the land is not rich. The plains along the coast are narrow and do not provide much farmland either. The Yucatán Peninsula is flat, but the soil is very poor.

Mexico has great mineral wealth. Almost every known mineral, including gold, silver, coal, oil, and natural gas, can be found there. It is the world's leading producer of silver, and it is one of the top ten producers of petroleum.

The Tropic of Cancer crosses through the center of Mexico. Because of this, most of the country is in the tropical zone. The mountains provide relief from the heat, however, with temperatures being cooler in the highlands. Temperatures at sea level are very warm all year. The Isthmus of Tehuantepec, south of the Sierra Madre del Sur, is an area of flatter land that is covered with tropical rain forests.

History. Unlike the northern countries, Mexico had several important civilizations *before* the arrival of the Europeans. The Maya (mä'yə) were a great civilization on the Yucatán Peninsula and the Isthmus of Tehuantepec during the first thousand years after Jesus died. The Aztecs had a powerful empire whose capital was at Tenochtitlán, now Mexico City, beginning in the 1300s.

Both the Aztecs and the Maya built huge stone pyramids, created beautiful jewelry and stone statues, and otherwise decorated their magnificent cities. The Maya empire had ended before Columbus. The Aztecs, however, were still powerful in the early 1500s and were conquered by the Spanish in 1519.

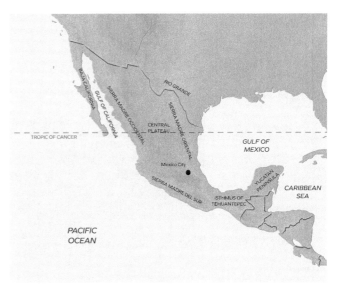

| Mexico

The Spanish did not settle the land to live as farmers, like colonists in the northern countries. They came instead as conquerors and set up large **estates** run by Indian slaves. Spain ruled the country harshly, and took much of Mexico's great mineral wealth to Europe. The Spanish people born in Mexico, as well as the Indians began to resent the mother country's harsh rule. They succeeded in winning independence in 1821, after a long struggle.

| Mayan pyramid at Chichen Itza

For a hundred years after independence Mexico was in **turmoil**. The country had many emperors, presidents, wars, and rebellions. Finally, from 1910 to 1920, a huge rebellion called "The Revolution" broke out against the powerful and cruel masters of Mexico. When it was over, Mexico had an elected president and a constitution. They have elected their leaders ever since that time.

Today. Mexico is beginning to be a manufacturing nation, but most of the people are still very poor. The Spanish conquest set up a system of very rich people running the country and very poor doing the work. That is changing, but mostly still true. The government tried to fix the problem by running many of its businesses the same way as in communist countries, but that made things worse. The government now is encouraging people to run the businesses and help Mexico grow into a more prosperous nation for all its people.

Answer these questions.

3.1   What is the capital of Mexico? _____

3.2   Mexico's culture and people are a mixture of what two groups?

_____

3.3   What is the name used for all the mountains of the cordillera in Mexico?

_____

3.4   What is the heartland of Mexico? _____

3.5   What isthmus and peninsula are flat land in Mexico?

_____

_____

3.6   What are two minerals that Mexico is a world leader in producing?

_____

3.7   What are the names of the two great civilizations in Mexico before the arrival

of the Europeans? _____

3.8   When did Mexico become independent from Spain? _____

3.9   What happened in Mexico from 1910 to 1920?

_____

Central America

Belize, Guatemala, El Salvador, Honduras, Nicaragua, Costa Rica, and Panama are the
seven countries of Central America. You will need to recognize the names as being Central
American countries, but you will not need to locate them except on the following map.

Central America is the bridge of land between North and South America. It is
geographically part of North America. It is a land of steep mountains and volcanoes.

3.10   Using an atlas, encyclopedia, or online resources, label each country in Central America. Put a dot on the map where each capital is located and label it.

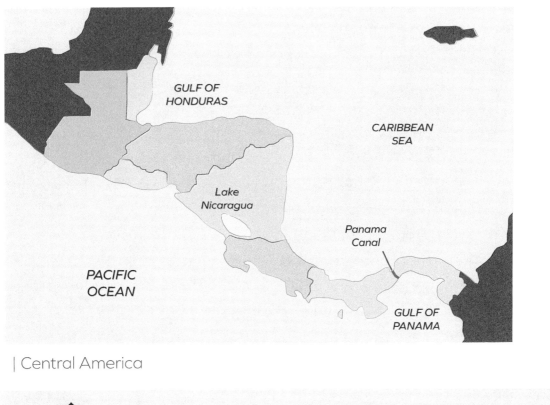

GULF OF
HONDURAS

CARIBBEAN
SEA

Lake
Nicaragua

Panama
Canal

PACIFIC
OCEAN

GULF OF
PANAMA

| Central America

Teacher check:

Initials _____   Date _____

The people of Central America come mostly from two different groups: Native Americans and Europeans.(There is also a smaller group of Africans.) The countries of the region have different mixes of these three groups. For example, most of the people of Costa Rica are of European descent, while in Guatemala the people are about half Indian and half mestizo (European/Indian mix). Belize has the largest African population, descendants of slaves brought in to work the plantations around the Caribbean Sea. The culture of the region is mainly a mix of Indian and Spanish.

Geography. The cordillera continues all the way to Panama, covering most of the land. There is a very narrow strip of coastal plains on the Pacific side of the mountains and a wider plain on the Atlantic side. The mountains divide the countries, making communication and trade between the Pacific and Atlantic coasts difficult.

There are over a hundred volcanoes among the Pacific coast mountains of Central America, at least fourteen of which are still active. This is one of the most active volcanic areas in the Western Hemisphere. The eruptions there have spread ash and made the west coast soil very rich. So, in spite of the dangers from the volcanoes and the earthquakes that go with them, most of the people of Central America live along the Pacific coast.

The Atlantic plains receive almost twice as much rain as the opposite coast. Much of the Atlantic side is covered with rain forest, which makes very poor farmland. There are many rivers that run from the mountains into the Atlantic which can be traveled by riverboats. The Pacific side has fewer, shorter rivers. The Pacific rivers come down steeply to the ocean and usually cannot be navigated by boats for very long distances.

History. Central America, along with south Mexico, was the home of the Mayan civilization in the first thousand years after Christ. These people built beautiful stone cities, wrote books, charted the stars in the sky, and made an accurate calendar. The Maya had lost their power by the time the Europeans came at the beginning of the 1500s. Their culture lives on though, among the Indians of the region.

Most of Central America was under Spanish rule after the arrival of the Europeans. Belize was the only exception; it became a British colony. Spanish Central America became independent in 1821. The region tried to unite as a single country, but the different states fought with each other and split apart. Since independence, the countries have tried to reunite several times and failed.

Panama was a part of the South American country of Colombia when it became independent from Spain in 1821. Panama became a separate country when the U.S. wanted to put a canal through the country to connect the Pacific and Atlantic Oceans. Colombia would not accept the U.S. offer for the land needed to build it, so the U.S. helped Panama become independent and the new government allowed the canal to be built.

| The Panama Canal connects the Pacific Ocean to the Atlantic Ocean.

The countries of Central America have not been very stable. They have had many dictators, civil wars, and military takeovers of the government. Such problems have made it difficult for business to make money and people to get jobs. The lack of jobs and businesses has kept the people poor.

Today. Central America is a very poor part of the world. Very few minerals are found there, so there is very little manufacturing. Most of the countries' exports are crops, like coffee, sugar, cotton, and bananas. Panama does have the canal, which came completely under its control in the year 2000. (In 1903, a treaty gave the U.S. the right to build and operate the canal.) The many ships that pass through it pay tolls to the government. But the biggest challenge for the governments is to elect honest individuals and build better lives for their people.

Answer these questions.

3.11 The people of Central America are descended mainly from what two groups?
_____

3.12 Most of Central America is covered with what? _____

3.13 Which are wider—the Pacific coast plains or the Atlantic?
_____

3.14 What makes the soil rich along the Pacific coast, but also makes it dangerous to live there? _____

3.15 What covers much of the Atlantic coast plains? _____

3.16 What great civilization was in Central America before the Europeans came?
_____

3.17 What European country ruled most of Central America? _____

3.18 Why did Panama become independent from Colombia?

_____

_____

3.19 What are the main exports of Central America? _____

West Indies

The West Indies are thousands of islands east of Mexico and Central America around the Caribbean Sea. They are divided into two major archipelagoes: the Bahamas and the Antilles. The Antilles are divided into the larger islands of the *Greater Antilles*, north of the Caribbean Sea, and the smaller *Lesser Antilles*, east of the Caribbean. These islands were the first part of North America discovered by Columbus. They were named the Indies because the great explorer thought he was near India.

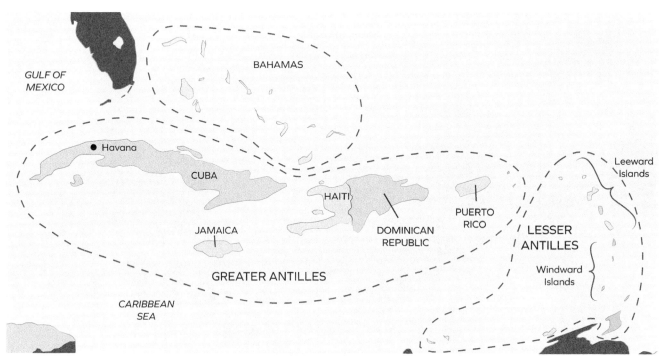

| West Indies

The people of the West Indies are mainly a mix of African and European. Their ancestors came from many different European countries or were brought over as slaves to work the large plantations set up by the Europeans. There is also a small population of Asians, mostly from the areas of India or China. The Native Americans who lived on the islands before the time of Columbus died of diseases or were killed by the Europeans.

Geography. The islands of the West Indies are the tops of a chain of mountains that run under the ocean between North and South America. The islands often have mountain ranges in the center. Many of the islands were formed by volcanoes, some of which are still active. Coral reefs are common around the islands, and some of the smaller islands are made of coral.

The Greater Antilles are the largest islands in the West Indies. They are the islands of Cuba, Hispaniola, Jamaica, and Puerto Rico. The Lesser Antilles includes a northern group called the *Leeward Islands* and a southern group called the *Windward Islands*. There are also some islands along the coast of South America that are part of the Lesser Antilles, such as Aruba and the Netherlands Antilles.

The Antilles Archipelago is all south of the Tropic of Cancer, in the tropical zone. That means that the temperatures would normally be hot all year. However, since these are islands, the ocean and winds cool them down somewhat. Also, since there are mountains on many of the islands, it is cooler up in the high lands. The islands' temperatures are mostly in the high 70s or low 80s (24° to 27° C). There is usually enough rainfall for the people, and some of the mountainsides get so much rain that rain forests are made. Hurricanes are a danger during the season from June to November.

History. The West Indies were home to several Indian tribes when Columbus discovered them in 1492. In the years that followed, thousands of Europeans from many nations came to the islands in search of gold and wealth. The Spanish set up the first successful European settlement in America in the West Indies. They founded the city of Santo Domingo on Hispaniola in 1496.

Spanish, British, French, Dutch, and Danish people settled on the islands to claim them for their governments, so the islands were controlled by many different countries. The Europeans discovered that sugar cane could be grown on the islands at a good profit. The Indians on the islands died of European diseases or were worked to death on farms or in mines. After that, millions of African slaves were brought in to work the fields of the new plantations.

| Sugarcane plants

In 1802 the island of Hispaniola became the first island to gain its independence. The African people there successfully revolted against France, which controlled that island. The new nation split to form the Dominican Republic and Haiti, the two nations that still share the island.

Slavery was ended in the West Indies by the end of the 1800s. After that time, the Europeans began to lose interest in these islands. Also, the United States was becoming more powerful, and it did not like European colonies so close. In 1898, the Americas helped Cuba become independent and took over Puerto Rico in the Spanish-American War. In 1917, the U.S. purchased the Virgin Islands from Denmark. After World War II (1938-1945), many of the islands either became independent or were given more control over their own affairs.

Today. There are thirty territories in the West Indies today. As of 2015, seventeen were colonies or territories of another country and thirteen were independent nations. Haiti, the Dominican Republic, and Cuba are the only nations with a long history of independence. Most of the rest separated from their mother countries after World War II.

The islands that are still colonies do not want to be independent. Some of the island nations like Anguilla and Montserrat are too small to survive without help. Usually the colonies have a government on the island that takes care of their own problems. They are content to let the larger mother country give them aid and take care of the more expensive world problems. The people in the U.S. territories of Puerto Rico and the U.S. Virgin Islands have never voted in favor of independence.

The West Indies is a very poor region. The U.S.-owned island of Puerto Rico has the most manufacturing and makes most of its money that way. There are few mineral resources on any of the islands except for Trinidad, which has large amounts of petroleum, making it the richest nation of the islands. But farming is still the most important way to make a living on most of the islands.

The second most important industry of the islands, after farming, is tourism. The warm climate, beautiful beaches, lush mountains, and colorful coral reefs of the West Indies attract many visitors. People from the wealthier, cooler nations of North America find it especially easy to visit these nearby, lovely islands.

| Stingray City on Grand Cayman allows interaction with stingrays.

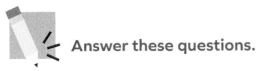

Answer these questions.

3.20   What are the two archipelagoes of the West Indies?

_____

3.21   What are the four islands of the Greater Antilles?

_____

3.22   What are the names of the two island groups in the Lesser Antilles?

_____

3.23   The people of the West Indies are descendants of what two groups?

_____

3.24   What was the first successful European settlement in America?

_____

3.25   How many countries are there in the West Indies?

_____

3.26   What is the most important way the islanders make a living?

_____

Answer _true_ or _false_.

3.27   _____   Spain ruled all of the islands of the West Indies.

3.28   _____   Some of the West Indies are still colonies.

3.29   _____   The West Indies were the part of North America first discovered by
Columbus.

3.30   _____   There are many mountains on the islands.

3.31   _____   Most of the nations of the West Indies that became independent
did so after World War II.

3.32   _____   Cuba was the first island to become independent.

3.33   _____   The people of the West Indies are rich because of the many
mineral resources on the islands.

Before you take this last Self Test, you may want to do one or more of these self checks.

1. _____ Read the objectives. See if you can do them.
2. _____ Restudy the material related to any objectives that you cannot do.
3. _____ Use the **SQ3R** study procedure to review the material:
    a. **S**can the sections.
    b. **Q**uestion yourself.
    c. **R**ead to answer your questions.
    d. **R**ecite the answers to yourself.
    e. **R**eview areas you did not understand.
4. _____ Review all vocabulary, activities, and Self Tests, writing a correct answer for every wrong answer.

SELF TEST 3

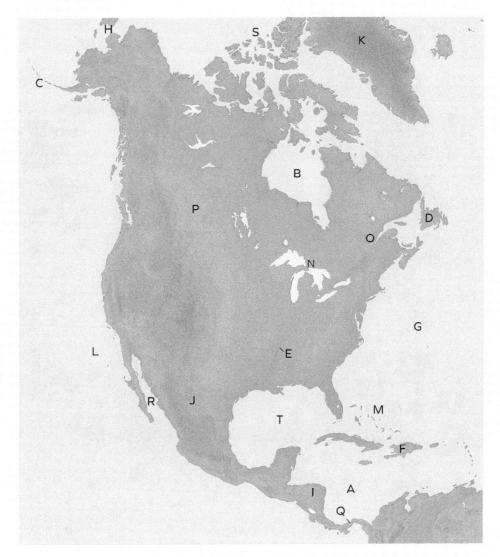

Choose the best letter for each feature, country, or region. Each is used only once (3 points each answer).

3.01	_____ Canada	**3.02**	_____ Bering Strait
3.03	_____ Mississippi River	**3.04**	_____ Aleutian Islands
3.05	_____ Gulf of Mexico	**3.06**	_____ Mexico
3.07	_____ Bahama Islands	**3.08**	_____ Caribbean Sea
3.09	_____ Great Lakes	**3.010**	_____ Atlantic Ocean
3.011	_____ Hudson Bay	**3.012**	_____ Queen Elizabeth Islands

3.013	_____	St. Lawrence River	3.014	_____	Newfoundland
3.015	_____	Antilles Islands	3.016	_____	Greenland
3.017	_____	Central America	3.018	_____	Pacific Ocean
3.019	_____	Isthmus of Panama	3.020	_____	Gulf of California

Put the letter for the correct country or region beside each statement. *W* is for the West Indies, *C* for Central America, and *M* for Mexico (2 points each answer).

3.021	_____	The important mountains are called the Sierra Madre.
3.022	_____	Seven countries are in the region; six were Spanish colonies.
3.023	_____	Cuba, Puerto Rico, Trinidad
3.024	_____	Belize, Honduras, Nicaragua
3.025	_____	Mayan <u>and</u> Aztec civilizations
3.026	_____	Leeward and Windward Islands
3.027	_____	a central plateau surrounded by mountains and narrow coastal plains
3.028	_____	Volcanoes made the Pacific coast soil rich; most of the people live there.
3.029	_____	has no coastline on the Pacific Ocean
3.030	_____	area Columbus first discovered in North America

Answer *true* or *false* (1 point each answer).

3.031	_____	The Great Basin is a desert in the Canadian Shield.
3.032	_____	The Mason-Dixon Line separates the U.S. and Mexico.
3.033	_____	Alberta, Manitoba, and British Columbia are part of the West Indies.
3.034	_____	The Great Plains are an important wheat- and grain-growing area.
3.035	_____	Baffin Island is the largest island on earth.
3.036	_____	Mexico has great mineral wealth.
3.037	_____	The people and culture of Mexico are a mix of Inuit and African.

3.038 _____ The people of the West Indies are a mix of African and European.

3.039 _____ The cordillera in North America runs from Alaska to Panama.

3.040 _____ Mexico was a colony of Denmark.

3.041 _____ There are rain forests in southern Mexico and Central America.

3.042 _____ The St. Lawrence Seaway allows ocean ships to travel to the Great Lakes.

3.043 _____ Most of Greenland is covered by an ice cap.

3.044 _____ The Isthmus of Techuantepec is in Canada.

3.045 _____ Central America connects North America with Asia.

3.046 _____ The contiguous states in the U.S. include Alaska and Hawaii.

3.047 _____ Central America is covered with mountains.

3.048 _____ Canada is a member of the British Commonwealth.

3.049 _____ The U.S., Canada, and Mexico are all federal republics.

3.050 _____ North America is the largest continent on earth.

Teacher check:

Score _____

Initials _____

Date _____

80 / 100

Before you take the LIFEPAC Test, you may want to do one or more of these self checks.

1. _____ Read the objectives. See if you can do them.
2. _____ Restudy the material related to any objectives that you cannot do.
3. _____ Use the **SQ3R** study procedure to review the material.
4. _____ Review activities, Self Tests, and LIFEPAC vocabulary words.
5. _____ Restudy areas of weakness indicated by the last Self Test.

NOTES

NOTES